LINKS

Scan the QR code or visit https://linktr.ee/insta.aesthetic to open all the links mentioned in the book (bonus included!)

TABLE OF
Content

01
Intro

02
Be inspired

03
The formula

04
The dirty secret

05
6-steps strategy

ABOUT THIS
Book

Each year I take countless courses to grow my digital skills.
Unfortunately, most of those courses are not as good as I expected. The major problem that I face is the complete lack of actionable information. They keep everything very vague.
That is why I wrote this book. This book contains all the information that I wanted to have in those courses.
A clear, systematic guide that tells you exactly how to make things.
Moreover, it explains how to go from point A to point B, without giving you any general information that you do not know how to apply.
Each step has an exercise that will help you **achieve your goal easier and faster**.

Remember: complete all the exercises before going to the next step and don't forget to share your results on our Facebook group along the way!

Are you excited to get started? I AM!

LET'S CONNECT

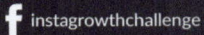 instagrowthchallenge   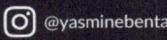 @yasminebenta

CHAPTER

01
Intro

INTRO

01

The importance of a clean feed

"What eyes can see, reaching more for what the heart can feel"
- Asiyami Gold, travel blogger & storyteller

I could not agree more with this quote.
Images are universal and so are stories, and **the way we tell our stories through images** is what opens up new and exciting opportunities to connect with our audience.

Today establishing our brands no longer relies only on traditional forms of media.
Now we can implement online content strategies that demand attention using readily available platforms.
However, with each new medium, **a new form of narrative arises**.
Instagram has its own and to build your brand, you need to master it.
You need to find your **visual voice**.

INTRO

The importance of a clean feed

01

"Images are universal and so are stories"

The concept of **"Aesthetic"** is the fundamental of Instagram.
If your pictures are ugly then all the growth strategies that you will follow are not going to work for you.
This book will help you **find your visual voice** and create a beautiful, **aesthetically pleasing feed.**

If you are reading this book now, you have recognized that we are living in a time when regular people are creating their dream lives from scratch, by following and sharing their passions. Small brands are transforming into global empires.

You too can be part of this by learning how to share your stories and help people achieve their goals.

Inspiration

CHAPTER

02

Your limitation—it is only your imagination

The primary steps in creating a consistent Instagram feed are:

- Developing your sense of aesthetic
- To be inspired

Inspiration is the key that will guide you in transforming your feed beautifully and uniquely.

How to do that?

EXERCISE

Create a Pinterest board where you will pin all the screenshots of all the instagram accounts that you love.
My suggestion here is to leave your creativity flowing.
You only have two rules to follow:

a) The feeds should be somehow related to your niche (e.g. If your niche is related to natural beauty, then you cannot include an account in the travel niche)
b) Include only the feeds that you find visually pleasing.

Here is mine: Pinterest board - account inspo

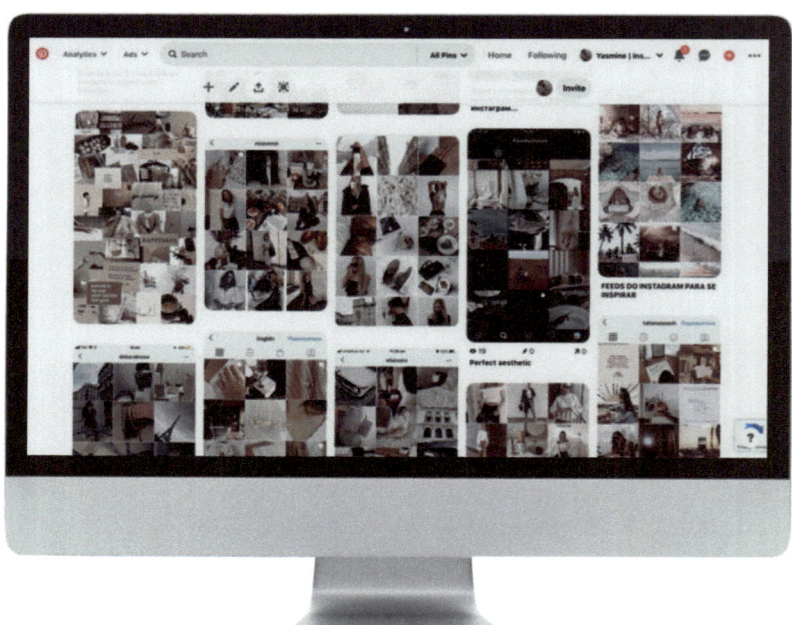

EXERCISE:

After putting together at least **10 different feeds**, choose the **two feeds that you like the most**.
Start analyzing the type of content that is shared, by replying to these three questions:

a) Why I love them?
b) Why I follow them?
c) What kind of pictures do they share?

Let us do this together.
These are the two Instagram feeds that I like the most.
They match my aesthetic and they are related to my niche.

Brand   Influencer

@_STORIESSTUDIO   @JANICEJOOSTEMA

The three questions

01
Why I love them?

I like the clean and organized look. I am in love with the colors, and the vibes and everything feels just perfect together.

02
Identify the UVP (why you follow them):

@_storiesstudio
Creative inspiration. They share beautiful and inspiring videos of how they made a
particular logo. I am learning their design processes every day; that is why I follow them.

@janicejoostema
Janice shares her looks in a very aesthetic way. I love her feminine and modern style; she inspires me on how to dress beautifully.

03
What kind of pictures do they share?

@_storiesstudio
Logos and branding, editorial pictures, travel pictures.
@janicejoostema
Outfits, makeup, product/detail pictures, interior design.

Do you start seeing the pattern?
They both stick to this kind of pictures; they are not posting anything else but these images, and that is what attracts their followers.

However, I want you to ask yourself another question.

WHY DO THEIR FEEDS LOOK SO PUT TOGETHER AND CONSISTENT?

CHAPTER

03
The formula

THE FORMULA

03

How to create your feed

"You are art."

STEP #1:
MOOD & COLORS

Based on the two Instagram accounts that you like the most, you should define your theme, which is the result of the overall mood and colors that you want your future feed to have.
Imagine your Instagram theme as your visual personality.

Here is a list of different instagram accounts with completely different themes that you can take into considerations when finding your own style:

- **@asiyami.gold** (travel + stories),
- **@storiesstudio** (creative + agency),
- **@k.els.ey** (minimal fashion),
- **@charlotteemilysanders** (no filter fashion),
- **@kkwbeauty** (beauty brand)

Choose your main colors

It is also imperative to choose about three primary colors, which will guide you when it comes to taking pictures because if you have seven or eight different colors in your feed, it is not going to have a cohesive color or tone.

You can find your color inspiration on Pinterest, by searching "**color palette**".

EXERCISE
Define the mood and three primary colors for your feed.
Mine are given below:

Mood: *clean aesthetic*
Colors: *beige, black, white*

STEP #2:
FIND YOUR NICHE

I have been struggling with finding a niche for ages on my personal profile.
I have switched from fashion to travel posts without any consistency.
I kept loosing followers because they were more confusing than me about my actual content!
If your feed is a mess too, then it is time to decide which niche you should be in.

However, what is a *niche*?
A niche market is a segment of a broader market that can be defined by its own unique needs, preferences, or identity.
Why choosing a niche?
In a niche there is less competition and higher possibilities of exponential growth.

Travel, beauty, design, and fashion are not niches.
They are MEGA HUGE topics.
You need to narrow them to find the right direction.
For example, a niche definition should look like this:

- Travel on a budget tips for a family of four
- Natural beauty DIY tutorial
- Second-hand luxury fashion for women under 30

These are niches. You can get creative here.
Let yourself be inspired by Pinterest, other Instagram account, understand what you like and how you can deep dive into a specific topic.
Once you have found 2-3 niches that you like, start research about them, you need to be sure they are profitable.

DEFINE YOUR UVP
If you do not have a marketing background, this word can be tricky for you.
UVP means **UNIQUE VALUE PROPOSITION**, and to apply this concept to the Instagram world, we can translate it as "WHY PEOPLE SHOULD FOLLOW ME". What is the value that you bring to your followers?
It is not all about pretty pictures anymore. You need to have a clear strategy about how you want to attract your followers according to your niche.

Repeat with me: WHY PEOPLE SHOULD FOLLOW ME?
For example, if you are in the natural beauty niche, the answer to this question could be "because I share 30sec videos on how to handmade cosmetics with natural ingredients and people will learn something new every day".
That is cool, isn't it?
Again, you do not need to invent anything here.

See what others are doing and make the best out of what famous influencers are doing. Capitalize their knowledge and take advantage of analyzing their large engagements to see which answer is better than another is.

THE 5-MINUTES FORMULA
Still do not know how to find your niche?

This was a real game-changer for me, and I hope it will help you too.

Once you have defined who you are, you can use this formula to define your niche and purpose better.

It works like this: **Niche = who you help + how you help them + your unique lens or world view**

For example:

Natural beauty niche:
(Who you help) *I help young women with oily skins who do not want to wear a lot of make* up.
(How you help them) *By sharing short videos on how to DIY cosmetics from natural ingredients.*
(Unique lens) *Because chemical ingredients contained in drug store products are the main causes of bad skin and acne. When I shifted to natural cosmetics, my skin started to look a lot better!*

For me:
I help young humans who want to build an independent location business by sharing online marketing tips and tricks to create the life they want to live. Life is too short to be stuck into a job that you are not passionate about.

Now it is your turn!
What is your niche?

EXERCISE
Define your niche + UVP using the 5-mins formula!

STEP #3: CONTENT CATEGORIES & ROTATION

At this point, you have defined:
- Your theme
- Your niche
- Your UVP

It is time to understand which type of content you are going to post. You need to categorize your photos.

Categories are topics that can be related to your business or lifestyle. They might be things with direct associations that relate to your products or services, or something associated with your brand or personality.

The famous youtuber Kelsey Simone categorizes her pictures into:
- Selfies
- Outfit pictures
- Product shots
- Fillers

Then it is all about **rotating them**! For example, if you post a selfie, you do not want to post another selfie right after that; instead, you need to develop your pattern.

So you will post a selfie, a product shot, an outfit picture, a filler, and keep that going.

If you are a brand and selling natural products, then your categories could be:

- Product shots
- Ingredients
- Recipe
- Tutorial
- People using your products
- Testimonial

Try to think like your ideal follower/client; what would you want to see?

Let us analyze the pattern of Janice Joostema:

interior – outfit – selfie
outfit – interior – selfie
interior – selfie – detail
outfit –product – outfit
outfit – selfie – interior

See how she keeps her feed so clean.

EXERCISE:
Define 3 to 5 post categories

STEP #4:
NEGATIVE SPACES AND FILLERS

One of the key elements to getting an aesthetic feed is having a lot of negative space pictures and fillers.
Look at those travel and interior design pictures of Janice. They keep telling the story of the brand, and they represent the aesthetic of the influencer, but the most important function that they have is that they create space.
Fillers give your feed an organized look and feel.

Client: @mynameiszurich

EXERCISE

Create a Pinterest board with fillers pictures related to the post categories that you choose.
Mine: Pinterest board - fillers

STEP #5:
POSES

Learning how to be confident beyond the camera is crucial to be more photogenic and take better pictures.
How to do that?
Plan in advance.
Once you have categorized your pictures, it is so important to understand that you can have a different type of pictures for each category.
Bear with me.

To create a more dynamic feed, you should work on:
- rotating different **photo categories** (see step #3)
- rotating different **poses** for each **category**

Let me explain better.
See the Janice Joostema feed, how many different poses for selfies she has?
I can see four.

My suggestion here is to create another Pinterest board called "**Instagram poses**" or "**Instagram post ideas**".
Inside this board, you will create different sections; one for each photo category that you have chosen (including fillers).
Inside each section, pin all the poses that you like. You can save your images directly from Instagram or by searching on Pinterest.

EXERCISE
Create a Pinterest board called "Instagram poses" or "Instagram post ideas" (if you are a brand) and create different sections.
Remember, the more pictures you pin, the better.

Mine: Pinterest board - Instagram post ideas

STEP #6:
TAKE YOUR NEW PICTURES

Choose 9 to 12 pictures in your Pinterest board. It is time to **COPY WITH PRIDE**!
Take your time and start **re-taking the pictures you choose**. However, at this time, you will be the model!
Play with different poses, put your phone on a tripod and use the auto-shutter.
Use the "**live photo**" feature on iPhone to have more pictures to choose from.
Practice repeatedly until you are satisfied with your pictures (they need to be as similar as possible).

You can also use some of your old pictures to replace some of the images that you chose if they are similar.

INSPIRATION	MY VERSION

EXERCISE
Take 9 to 12 pictures

STEP #7:
FILTERS

A theme is nothing without a filter.
Using the same filter/settings on your photos, all the time, is the easiest way to start a theme.
Imagine your filter as your **signature look.**

I use Lightroom to edit my pictures, but if you are just starting out then you can choose one of the filters that I saved here. They all work with **VSCO**!

BONUS TIME!
Download VSCO and find in my Pinterest board - filters 50+ VSCO recipes that you can use to edit your pictures!

Although editing a picture with the same filter will not always guarantee a perfect result.
What to do when it happens?
You need to work with collateral settings.
Apply your filter/preset, and then start experimenting with lights, contrast, shadows, white and color balance to reach your perfect result!

Sometimes even working with collateral settings cannot lead to the result you have wished for. When it happens, go for black & white (if your theme has these colors) or delete the picture.

Deleting your pictures is definitely something you want to avoid, but if you took your photo in very different light conditions, then the only thing you can do is paying much more attention when shooting next time.

  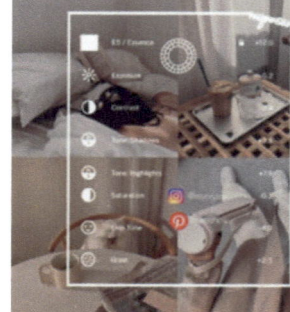

EXERCISE
Choose one of the VSCO recipes and edit the pictures you've already taken!

STEP #8:
REARRANGE THE ORDER OF YOUR PHOTOS TO MAKE YOUR FEED FLOW

At this stage, you know what you want your overall theme to look like.
You know what you want to post about.
Moreover, you have a filter.
Perfect!
Your feed is starting to look really good!

Now, you need to make it flow.
The trick is to **rearrange the order of your posts to create balance** and being sure your feed is **not too busy** or cluttered.
You want to make sure **it is easy for new eyes to move throughout your feed** without interruption. The goal here is to create a *depth of field*. How to do this?

Place busier photos next to clean or minimal photos ("fillers") to break things up a bit.

Client: @simonespaccatore

I use Preview to rearrange the order of posts and to see what my Instagram feed will look like before I post it on Instagram.
Just upload your photos / videos / albums in the app and drag and drop to move them around.
If a photo does not fit, just delete it from your Preview feed.

Client: @mynameiszurich

To know which photo you should put next to each other, follow the pattern that you define in Step 3. Rearranging your feed is all about balance.
Avoid putting photos that are too similar next to each other. Space them out.

By spacing out photos that are too similar, you can create contrast between each post.
This will make your overall feed look balanced and professional.

EXERCISE
Download PREVIEW and rearranging your edited pictures to make your new feed flow.

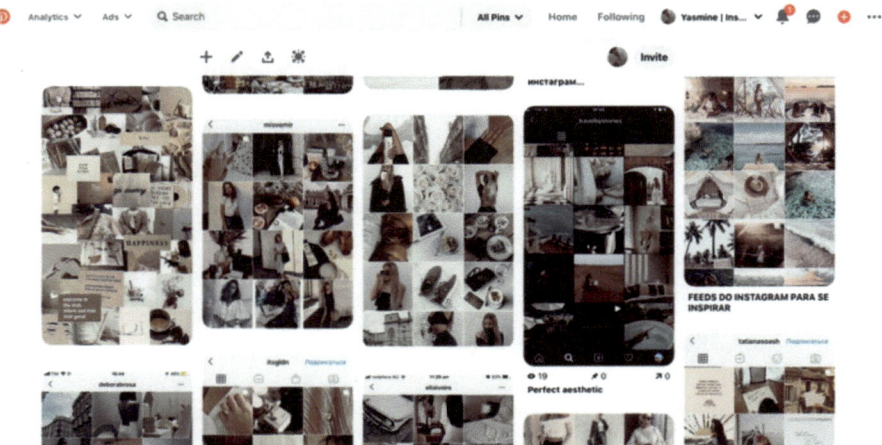

The dirty secret

CHAPTER

04

Discover the only dirty little secret of every successful brand and influencers are currently using for creating beautiful, consistent feeds and never running out of content.

If you are a brand/entrepreneur working on a tight marketing budget, commissioning custom content for your brand each month might be out of reach.
If you're an influencer, having something new to post each day can be exhausting.

So I am telling you the **greatest secret** that the most successful brands and influencers are hiding right now; **they all use stock pictures** to populate their feeds and **never** run out of content!

However, what are *stock photos*?
Stock photos are professionally shot images, videos, illustrations, and audio tracks that are purchased on a royalty-free basis.
When you purchase/download a piece of royalty-free content, you can use that content for nearly **any commercial project.**

Yes, I am saying that not all the pictures that influencers and brands post are actually "theirs". Although they are pretty good at finding good images that, fit their style, so you probably will not even notice the difference.

Mixing your content with stock pictures is an excellent recipe for a diverse and engaging feed for your audience. You just need to learn where to look for these images.

@missjoslin

@yasminechanel

In addition, of course, I got you covered!
Here are my favorite FREE stock pictures websites that I love and always use:

- Unsplash
- Pexels
- Pixabay

Yes, you do not need to pay an expensive subscription to Shutterstock to have beautiful stock images. Internet is the best place full of free resources if you know where to look!
However, how to use stock images the **right way**?
When looking for your pictures on those websites, you should look for images that:
- Could be you or representation of your brand
- Are native and aspirational to your audience
- Do not look overly curated or professional

DON'T USE THIS   USE THIS

CHAPTER

05
The 6-steps strategy

THE 6-STEPS STRATEGY

05

Planning, creating and executing your posts

At this point, you:

- Learnt what you want your feed to look like.
- Have a clear idea of the main topic of your Instagram account.
- Defined your category.
- Have a Pinterest board full of inspiration pictures.
- Shot 9-12 pictures.
- Found other beautiful pictures on Stock photo websites.

Now it is time to post!

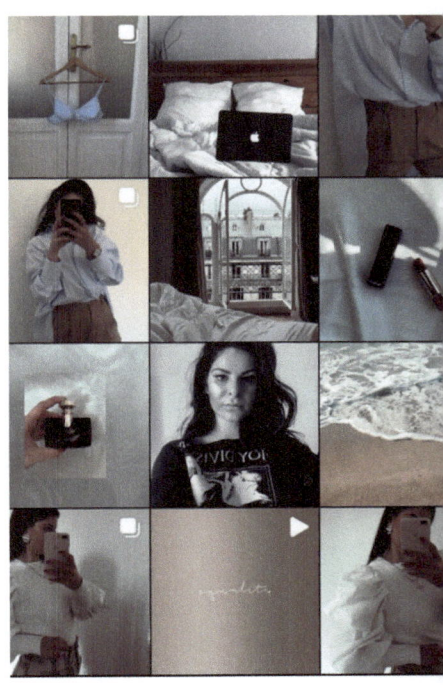

STEP #1:
HOW MANY POSTS WILL YOU CREATE EACH MONTH?

Instagram has changed, and even if the frequency of your posts is not as crucial as it was, **it is still essential to boost your engagement,** along with posting at least 5-10 stories per day and engage with other users.
So firstly, decide **how many times per week you want to post.**

Remember that you need to be consistent with posting, so choose a frequency that is comfortable for you.
Five posts per week can be a great start.
So you will need to prepare **20 posts to cover a full month (and two scrolls) of posting.**

STEP #2:
TAKE A LOOK AT YOUR CATEGORIES

In chapter 2, you defined your categories.
Remember: categories are topics that can be related back to your business.
It might be things with direct associations that relate to your products, services, or things associated with your brand.
If you need to plan for 20 posts, and you have five categories, then you need 4 posts per category.

Plan which pictures you need to take according to your categories.

STEP #3:
PLAN YOUR SHOOTING

I have a little secret to share that will help you have an obvious idea about what pictures you have to take or which content you should look for on stock pictures websites.

Do you remember **all the pictures that you save in your Instagram post inspiration board?**
Start from there.

My suggestion is to find the ideas for poses/style/mood of your next content straight from your Pinterest board (or across Instagram).

As we defined previously, we need four pictures for each category.
Start looking for pictures related to your categories on your boards and save them on your phone.

Once you have done that, open Preview and start organizing the pictures that you saved.

When you are happy with the overall aesthetic, you are ready for the next step.

STEP #4:
TAKE YOUR PICTURES

As we did in chapter 2, it is time to take your pictures or make your design!
At this time, we have more content to work on.

Remember to have fun; this is definitely the best part of the whole process.
Schedule the shootings in two days to be more efficient. Plan your location and all the outfits/tools that you will need.

Once you are ready, start making! Understand **which photos you need to take** and **which images you can download** from stock pictures websites.

Remember: you can always add more content during the month if you need to.
Although by making your pictures all together, you will always be sure to have all the posts you need.

STEP #5:
ORGANIZE YOUR FEED

Wow, you did a great job so far!
Open **Preview** and start replacing your photos inspiration with the one you took.
Can you see how beautiful your feed is now?

Remember to rotate categories and to post busier pictures close to clean images for a more organized look.

STEP #6:
WRITE YOUR CAPTIONS & SCHEDULE YOUR POSTS

Planning your feed means also **posting on purpose**.
It is important to **give value** in every post you make.
Take your time to **write all your captions**.

Remember to **tag brands** or **instagram pages** related to your niche for **maximize your exposure**!

Once you created all your captions, it is time to **schedule your posts**!

You can do that directly from Preview.
Preview will send you a notification when it is time to post.

Your new feed is ready!

From now on, you can focus on engaging with your audience, find new potential followers and customers on Instagram or Facebook group.

How great, right!

LET'S STAY
connected

Before we part ways, I want to let you know that this book is just the beginning of our conversation.
I invite you to continue the discussion by joining our new community!
A place where you can share your progress (even all the exercises you made while reading this book!), be supported by other like-minded people who cannot wait to support your journey and connect with you!
Join now the Facebook Group: INSTAGRAM GROWTH CHALLENGE - Boost your Instagram growth

Let's keep supporting one another by doing this together.
I sincerely want to **THANK YOU** for spending this time with me and letting me be your personal guide.
I wish you all the success you can dream of.

LET'S CONNECT

f instagrowthchallenge   ◉ @yasminebenta

www.ingramcontent.com/pod-product-compliance
Lightning Source LLC
Chambersburg PA
CBHW040338220526
45473CB00009B/2730